FROM AN ANT HILL SPRINGS A MOUNTAIN

FROM AN ANT HILL SPRINGS A MOUNTAIN

Barbara A. Pierce

From An Ant Hill Springs A Mountain by Barbara A. Pierce

ISBN 978-1-955136-08-2 (Paperback)
ISBN 978-1-955136-09-9 (Hardback)

This book is written to provide information and motivation to readers. Its purpose is not to render any type of psychological, legal, or professional advice of any kind. The content is the sole opinion and expression of the author, and not necessarily that of the publisher.

Copyright © 2021 by Barbara A. Pierce

All rights reserved. No part of this book may be reproduced, transmitted, or distributed in any form by any means, including, but not limited to, recording, photocopying, or taking screenshots of parts of the book, without prior written permission from the author or the publisher. Brief quotations for noncommercial purposes, such as book reviews, permitted by Fair Use of the U.S. Copyright Law, are allowed without written permissions, as long as such quotations do not cause damage to the book's commercial value. For permissions, write to the publisher, whose address is stated below.

Printed in the United States of America.

New Leaf Media, LLC
175 S. 3rd Street, Suite 200
Columbus, OH 43215
www.thenewleafmedia.com

CONTENTS

Why Read Lots Of Books 9
Happiness Is 11
Cleobald Jehosaphat 13
My Best Friend Teddy Bear 15
When Animals Speak 17
The Ritual 19
Tippity-tap Goes The Rain 20
Differences In People 21
The Pilgrims' Poem 23
Monsters Wouldn't Dare 25
Some Colors Of Nature 26
Snapshots 27
The Ostrich 29
My Dog Sparky, The Absolute Best 31
It's A Good Thing 33
It's Snowing Again 34
O' Little Skunk 37
Nature Recycles The Day 39
Bedtime Fears 41
There's A Mouse In My House 43
Mr. Appleby's Apple Obsession 45
Christopher Columbus 47
Just Silly Notions 49
Blue Jeans Are Popular 51
The Rustling Leaves 53
Let's Build A Snowman 55
It's A Blizzard After All 56
A Secret No More 57
The Night Of Halloween 59
Where Did The Good Manners Go 61
Frolicking In The Rain 62

How Minutes Morph	63
Samantha, The Class Bully	65
Friends Value Your Friendship	68
Giggle, Wiggle, Squirm and Jiggle	69
Big, Bold, Irregular Spots	71
The Olden Days	73
Not One, But Two	75
Proud Pigs	77
The Loch Ness Monster Speaks	79
The Crab In The Sand	81
The Water Cycle	83
Holiday Recollections	85
Limericks	87

Dedication and Acknowledgements

This book is dedicated to my uncle and aunt,
Leroy and Hattie Jones whose legacies are far reaching to this day.
Loving memories of both remain strong.

A special thanks to Keith Paris for giving his time and
technical expertise and to those who continue to support my work.

Why Read Lots Of Books

Reading lots of books is usually what

Smart kids do.

You can be just as smart if you would

Read some too.

Reading increases your knowledge and

Develops your mind.

A better way to succeed in life would

Definitely be hard to find.

Through books you can travel to many

A foreign land,

And be introduced to other cultures

You'll learn to understand.

Reading also can be just for fun

To wind down when all work

Is done.

Happiness Is . . .

Happiness is watching a television special all the way through

Without being told there's something else to do.

Happiness is slurping strands of spaghetti and meatballs

Without red sauce dribbling down your overalls.

Happiness is waking up on a school day and discovering you

Don't have to go

Due to a weather forecast of thirty-plus inches of snow.

Happiness is eating the last piece of chocolate cake to be had

Then finding out it was meant for your dad.

Happiness is eating all you wish

And not having to wash a single dish.

Happiness is hearing your teacher say, "You don't have to work

Today. You've already earned an A."

Happiness is eating a slice of apple pie a la mode

While imagining your brother's friends being chased by a toad.

Happiness is hearing that the class bully is leaving today.

Hurrah, let it be far, far north of the Milky Way!

Happiness is attending a school each day

Where the major subjects are eat, sleep, and play.

Happiness is always having a best friend around

Even if it is just the family's old toothless hound.

Cleobald Jehosaphat

Cleobald Jehosaphat was said to be

A real cool cat

Until he traded his nine lives

For a seedy old fisherman's hat.

How really cool was that?

Cleobald, a bit too late,

Realized he had sealed his fate.

Had he traded just one life, he would've

Been left with eight.

But he forgot one simple fact,

To always think before you act.

So reads the final epitaph of

Cleobald Jehosaphat,

Once said to be a real cool cat.

My Best Friend Teddy Bear

My best friend is my teddy bear.

I'm never lonely because he's always there.

Teddy listens to me day after day.

He never interrupts and never turns away.

I can tell he's interested in whatever I say

'Cause his eyes follow mine and never

Once begin to stray.

He doesn't laugh at me when I say dumb

Stuff.

He just sits until I've said enough.

No anger is ever shown with the weird

Things I say and do.

That's how I know he's a friend that's

True.

His soft expression belies only concern

And care,

Exactly what's expected from a real friend

Like TEDDY BEAR!

When Animals Speak

Dogs_ Bow wow Bow wow Bow wow.

Cats_ Meow Meow Meow.

Chicks_ Cheep Cheep Cheep and

Peep Peep Peep.

Birds _ Tweet Tweet Tweet.

Hens _ Cluck Cluck Cluck and

Puck Puck Puck.

Ducks _ Quack Quack Quack.

Geese _ Honk Honk Honk and

Clack Clack Clack.

Pigs _ Oink Oink Oink and

Oink Oink Oink.

Donkeys _ Hee-haw Hee-haw Hee-haw.

Crows _ Caw Caw Caw.

Cows _ Moo Moo Moo.

Roosters _ Cock-a-doo-dle-doo doo-dle-doo,

When animals speak.

The Ritual

A flock of birds nestles
Far above the ground
Waiting for the dawn of day
Barely making a sound.

When like magic
A sudden burst of sunlight
Ends the silence of the night.

The ritual begins with
Ease and grace
As each bird instinctively
Takes its place

Chirping jubilantly and fluttering
Wings
Welcoming the day and what
It brings.

Darting here and there
High and low
The birds pick and peck as
They go.

They find puddles in which to
Thrash about
Until each is satisfied and tires
Itself out.

As the day draws to an end
The flock starts to ascend
Back to the perch high up
Far above the ground
Waiting for the dawn of the next day
Barely making a sound.

Tippity-tap Goes The Rain

Tippity-tap Tippity-tap

Goes the rain on my window pane.

Tippity-tap Tippity-tap

It refuses to wane.

Tippity-tap Tippity-tap

It continues in the same vain.

Tippity-tap Tippity-tap

Tippity-tap Tippity-tap

Then slowly, tap tap tap.

You must hear it!__ tap tap tap

Differences In People

If everyone were alike,
Life would be a bore.

There would be very little
About anyone left to adore.

Those differences that make
Someone special would
Certainly not exist_

Only a life of mediocrity
Would surely persist.

Isn't it wonderful we're all
So unique_

Not only in personality, but
The entire physique!

Imagine the pleasures that lie
In wait_

Simply because differences
Make life great!

The Pilgrims' Poem

The Pilgrims traveled so far and so long

With only a hope, a prayer, and a song

Chances for a new beginning was what

They sought.

Triumph over evil winning was what they

Fought.

Never once did their spirits lack

The courage to go on and on.

No, there was no turning back!

They faced each challenge with strength

And will

With boundless patience and tremendous

Skill.

They were determined to reach that land

Where their dreams could abound and

Ultimately expand.

Monsters Wouldn't Dare

Monsters love to hear children scream and shout.

They really get a kick watching them run about.

The rascals know just who to bully and scare.

Bother me, In deed not, They wouldn't dare!

'Cause I'm not afraid of their weak old bluffs.

I'd just give 'um two or three backhand cuffs.

And if that's not enough__ I'd poke 'em right in the eyes

Just to get their attention and whittle them to size.

Then to be sure they bother no more,

I'd send them packing "POW" right through the door!

Some Colors Of Nature

BLUE is the sky up so high.
YELLOW is the sun. What a bright one.
GREEN is the grass in the fields I pass.
WHITE is the snow that falls softly below.
RED is the rose in which nectar grows.
PURPLE is the awesome sight of the horizon
Just before night.
ORANGE is the pumpkin on the ground:
Big, firm, plump, and round.
BLACK is the night in the radiance
Of the moonlight.
These are some colors of nature.

Snapshots

Snapshots

Capture the present

Soon to become the past

Merging time

That lingers in the future

Where the images last

And last and last.

The Ostrich

The big gray ostrich is a weird looking sight.
Though it flutters huge wings, it does not take flight.
Cumbersome and bulky describe the big fellow,
And has a disposition far from being mellow.
Its neck and legs are quite strong and tall
With a very little head on top of it all.
This flightless bird moves swiftly on the ground
If it becomes fearful when strangers come around.

My Dog Sparky, The Absolute Best

My Dog Sparky is a pale golden brown
And has a soft little face with a permanent frown.
Though his big ears dangle and hang really long,
They droop even more when he's done something Wrong.
He always chases the man that brings the mail
As he growls and barks and wags his scruffy tail.
Sparky is so energetic, he never sits still.
Just watching his antics gives me a big thrill.
Many friends refer to him as the wiggling pest,
But to me, SPARKY IS THE ABSOLUTE BEST!

It's A Good Thing

Wow! Look at that enormous brown snake

Slither up that old oak tree.

It's a good thing I spotted it first, before it spotted

Me!

It would have been quite a surprise, coming face to

Face with such piercing eyes!

Boy, did I move quickly to give it lots of space

And found myself another place.

Just imagine what might have been

If I had not just given in!

Who knows if that snake would have tried to pursue

Me as the main course of a lavish menu. WHEW!

It's Snowing Again

Snowing again!

Hope this is the

Last time,

Is the sentiment

Of some

Anxious to see it

All stop,

Wanting each falling

Flake to be the

Last drop,

While others take

A different view.

Snow makes everything

Sparkle like new.

An infectious hush veils

The land

Wherever the white, soft

Crystals stand.

The hustle and bustle

For a time will cease,

Spreading about serenity

And a sense of peace.

O' Little Skunk

O' little skunk black and white

You're often seen

In the dead of night

With your sad looking face

And small pointed nose

Aimed at the ground

Nearly touching your toes

While looking for something

Tasty to eat

Most often seeds, plants, or

An insect treat.

If you're approached

Or sense a threat

You then reveal

Your worst asset,

A very powerful and

Odious spray

That will take the

Intruder's breath away.

It's no wonder you have to

Go it alone

To forge for food all on your

Own.

Nature Recycles The Day

Last night's rain cleared the air

Of all the impurities that lurked up there.

Now, the sun's providing abundant light

To make another day clean, crisp, and bright.

Nature has a special way

Of recycling each passing day.

Bedtime Fears

When it's time for bed

And the lights go out

I imagine danger lurking about.

My mind conjures up frightening

Sights

Of crafty villains that rule the nights.

As the visions become more intense

Things that are happening make very

Little sense.

And before long, sleep appears

Just in time to erase all fears.

There's A Mouse In My House

There's a mouse in my house.

He keeps me jumping and chasing him about.

I want him out! I want him out!

He sneaks to my door

Then zips across the floor.

Grabbing anything near, I take careful aim.

He dodges my best efforts

As if playing a game.

I want him out! I want him out!

One day I'll succeed in getting the little pest.

Until then, catching him is my number one quest!

Mr. Appleby's Apple Obsession

Mr. Appleby calls his new puppy Apple Pie.

When he's often asked the reason why,

He smiles and answers proudly, "Because she is the apple

Of my eye!"

He was stunned when hearing a neighbor speaking to

Another, say

"Well, giving an animal a name like that, you know the

Man's strange anyway!"

Of course, Mr. Appleby felt that Apple Pie was the

Perfect name for his precious poodle!

Imagine their reaction if it were known he'd even

Considered Apple Crumb Cake, Apple Brown Betty,

And Dutch Apple Strudel

As possible names for his adored little poodle!

Christopher Columbus

Christopher Columbus sailed the Big Blue.

He took more than one ship _ more than two.

"Three small ones," said he

"And a crew of sailors to navigate the sea."

A tough group they were by all account

Until the time at sea began to mount

When the fear of the unknown set in

Mutiny entered the minds of many of the men.

When Columbus became aware of the fact

He reasoned with them and made a pact

Promising the rewards would be beyond great

If for a little while longer they would wait.

His plan was to reach India, a land rich with

Gold and spices,

A plan foiled by a storm, one of nature's

Devices.

The ships were blown off course and carried

A shore

To the little known island, San Salvador.

"Indians," said Columbus, referring to the

Inhabitants he met,

Unaware he had not reached the destination

On which his heart was set.

Just Silly Notions

Once I had the silly notion
To walk across the Atlantic Ocean,
But hurriedly changed my mind,
I couldn't leave my family BEHIND.

Then I thought about visiting China
By digging to the other side,
But discovered that Earth's as deep
As it is WIDE.

Blasting off for Mercury had some appeal
Before finding out about the extremes
I'd feel
Since the planet never turns,
One side freezes and the other side BURNS.

If only I could find Australia.
They say it's down under.
Down under what, I wonder?
Could it just be somewhere way out yonder?

Well, that's just another silly notion to
PONDER.

Blue Jeans Are Popular

Blue jeans are a familiar sight everywhere.

A real love for them, all seem to share.

In the past the styles and cuts were kind of

Tame.

Not so now, nothing's the same.

Belled, cuffed, cropped, or scalloped

Short, long, baggy, or tight

Whatever the style, it's quite all right.

Some prefer them faded

And others a little more dated.

The more daring go for the worn

Or jeans that are just plain torn.

Finding anyone with just one pair

Chances of that is extremely rare.

Their versatility and easy fit

Make them an overwhelming hit.

They can be dressed up or dressed

Down

Whether the occasion is a game,

A party, or merely a show in town.

The Rustling Leaves

The wind sends the leaves rustling down the street,

Cloaked in faded colors and irregular shapes,

Each leaf sending out a different beat

Crunching and crackling, as each escapes

To travel for just a short while

Then end up finally in some landfill pile.

Let's Build A Snowman

Let's build a snowman with a real personality,

A great big smile that mimics reality,

An orange carrot nose and two wide black eyes

To show he's alert and obviously wise,

One tall shiny muffed hat for his ears and head,

A scarf for his neck, the color fire engine-red.

Let's not forget some woolen mittens for his hands

To keep him comfortable for as long as he stands.

Oh what a handsome sight he'll make

Posing for pictures the neighbors come to take!

And to make certain he sticks around for a while,

We'll keep close watch on that thermometer's dial

For we know too soon we must voice our reluctant

Good-byes

Because inevitably the weather's temperature is going

To rise.

Then it's "So long for now Mr. Snowman.

When it snows next year, we'll build you again!"

It's A Blizzard After All

Twirling twirling twirling

Round and round

Kriss-cross kriss-cross

Down down down

Snowflakes are falling

To the ground.

A sea of white

Now covers the town.

Faster faster faster

The inches keep mounting.

Faster faster faster

The weatherman keeps counting.

Snow continues to fall.

Faster faster faster

It's a blizzard after all!

A Secret No More

A secret is just that,

A secret.

Information of which one is

Aware

But not meant to share

Because once it's out and passed

About

Nothing is the same as before.

The secret's a secret no more.

The Night Of Halloween

On the night of Halloween

Neighborhood children invade

The scene

Dressed as monsters, witches, and ghosts

Looking to frighten unsuspecting hosts

While bouncing in droves from door to door

Hoping to make a bountiful score.

First gesturing and BOOO-ING!

Then screeching and WHOOO-ING!

Finally, "Trick or treat, give me something

Good to eat!"

And when all the demands have been met,

On they go to bag more treasure yet.

When they've finished their raid on the town,

Home they go ready to settle down

While nibbling away at every single treat

Until all tummies have stretched and nothing's

Left to eat.

Then mommies and daddies take them to

Their beds

Rubbing growling tummies and holding aching

Heads.

Where Did The Good Manners Go

Please and Thank You,

Where did they go?

Does any one honestly know?

Excuse Me and I'm Sorry,

Are they missing in action too?

What a predicament! What are we

Going to do?

May I and Pardon Me

Have also left the fold

Though they've been heard in other

Places, so I've been told.

But still there is the desire to know

Right here and right now

Where Did The Good Manners Go?

Frolicking In The Rain

Frolicking about in the pouring rain

May seem to some a bit insane.

To children it tops the list

Of things most fun to do.

Of course such fun ends later

With AACHOO! AACHOO! AACHOO!

But since fun is a child's greatest priority

Why be concerned about a little infirmity?

Frolicking about in the pouring rain

Is so much fun to do

Even if later there's more AACHOO! AACHOO!

AAA__CHOOO! (Said louder and longer than the rest_)

How Minutes Morph

Let me sleep just one minute more

Before my feet hit the floor!

(a minute later)

Just one more minute is all I need

Then I'll do what I must indeed!

(a minute later)

One more minute I need right now

Surely, surely the time will allow!

(a minute later)

Just one minute is all I'm asking for

Then I'll head toward that door!

(a minute later)

One last minute till I open both eyes!

(a minute later)

My gosh, how time flies!

I hope those waiting for me to arrive

Know that one minute can morph

Into five.

Samantha, The Class Bully

Samantha, the class bully,

Sits deceptively calm

And at her best,

Pretending to blend in

With all the rest.

When the teacher's not looking

She picks classmates to harass,

Usually the most timid in the class.

As she proceeds in her annoying

Way

Whining and complaining set

The tone for the day.

When the teacher queries those in

Distress

Samantha's victims hesitate

Then confess

Her mean and cowardly deeds

At their expense

Have made them miserable and

Very tense.

The teacher insists that she leaves

Them alone,

Then contacts her parents by

Telephone.

The next day Samantha brings a note.

The following is the essence of

What her parents wrote.

Samantha will have no time for play

Since she wasted most of the day.

No visitors, no TV, no game,

For an entire week, more of the same.

After homework, dinner, then early

To bed.

No other words to her will be said.

She must understand the reasons

For such action

And change her unacceptable behavior

To our satisfaction.

It's in the positive things we want her

To participate,

Not to use the weaknesses of others

To bully and humiliate.

Our Samantha will be a new person

No doubt,

For we assure you the old one is on her

Way out!

SAMANTHA'S MOM and DAD

Friends Value Your Friendship

Friends accept you for who you are

Whether you are a passive soul

Or a brilliant star.

They see the good in you when it's

The best you can do.

They share the pride they see in you.

Friends will not be led a stray

By deceit or jealousy in any way.

Friends value your friendship.

Giggle, Wiggle, Squirm and Jiggle

Tickle tickle tickle

Makes some

Giggle giggle giggle

Giggle giggle giggle.

Tickle tickle tickle

Makes others

Giggle and wiggle

Giggle and wiggle.

Tickle tickle tickle

Makes me

Giggle, wiggle, squirm and jiggle

Giggle, wiggle, squirm and jiggle.

Tickle tickle tickle makes me

Giggle, wiggle, squirm and jiggle.

Big, Bold, Irregular Spots

There once was a giraffe

Whose name was really

Pun-jaffe.

He was as tall and handsome

As they come,

An opinion according to some.

Pun-jaffe hated his big, bold,

Irregular spots

Because there were lots and lots.

One day his eyes got such a gleam

For he had come up, he thought

With the perfect scheme.

After revealing what he had

Planned

His friends could not understand

Why he'd make such a

Ridiculous move

To believe on nature

He could improve!

In unison their responses were,

"Yipes, Yipes!

You would not look good as

A zebra does in stripes!

Are you aware that your big, bold,

Irregular spots enhance your

Distinctive look?"

Pointing this out and adding a

Bit of flattery was what it took

For Pun-jaffe to appreciate his

Beautiful spots.

He was now extremely happy

That nature had sprinkled him with lots

And lots

Of big, bold, beautiful, irregular

Spots!

The Olden Days

Grandparents often speak about the olden days

And how different things were in so many ways.

Foods and other products were delivered right to

The door

Or they could be purchased from a carry-all

General store.

Ice boxes for a time kept perishables quite cold

Both in the home and in the store where they were

Sold.

Prices of everything during that time sound

Surprisingly low

But people didn't make the same salaries long, long

Ago.

Just imagine, bread for a quarter and a coke for a

Dime.

Sounds unbelievable, even for that time!

They say many children made their own toys,

Baby dolls for the girls and go-carts for the boys.

A wide selection of fun activities kept the youth

Joyfully occupied.

On that, the grateful parents truly relied

As they looked on and cheered from the side

To make sure the rules of fair play were applied.

Not One, But Two

If you thought like I thought, you'd be me.

If I thought like you thought, I'd be you.

If we thought alike, we'd be one.

But we're two.

I'm me and you're you.

Not one, but two.

I can't be you and you can't be me.

We're yet a separate entity.

I'm me and you're you.

We're still not one, but two.

Proud Pigs

One very proud pig

Often boasted

How he could do

A jiggity-jig-jig

A jiggity-jig-jig

Until his hams

Got roasted.

No other proud pig

Has ever again boasted

How he could do

A jiggity-jig-jig

A jiggity-jig-jig

For fear of his

Rump being roasted.

The Loch Ness Monster Speaks

A surprise sighting of Nessie on the Loch Ness yesterday

Was far less frightening than previous spotters say.

Prehistoric in appearance, of course

Being the last of the great dinosaurs

Stranded in the Loch Ness for millions of years

Stemming volumes of curiosity and heightening

Fears.

Today, she sent a message for all pursuers

To heed

Before continuing on her two-mile-wide lead.

The giant reptile bellowed warnings that she wishes to

Be left alone

And that the Scottish loch will remain her home

For perhaps another million years,

Then she will relocate to a lake somewhere in the

French Algiers.

The Crab In The Sand

Near the water's edge, Eloise spies a crab in the sand,

A hermit crab, small enough to fit inside of her hand

Sideling along with a burden on top of its back,

A shell to perhaps serve as a temporary shack.

Eloise thinks the shell is much too heavy for it to bear

But the diminutive creature continues to lug it, while

At Eloise stare

For as long as she stands motionlessly by

Simply gazing at it eye to eye.

For quite some time the struggle persists through

Untrodden sand

Until, without any warning, showers begin pelting

Over sea and over land

Prompting Eloise to shield her eyes and tilt down her

Head

The same moment the crab wriggled down in the

Sand and fled

Leaving the heavy oversized burden behind,

A welcomed sight for Eloise who sees it as

A fantastic find

Because of the fond memories of that day in the

Sand

And the amazing friend she met that could fit in

Her hand.

The Water Cycle

Water makes its rounds

Sometimes up, sometimes down.

Be it rain, snow, sleet, or hail

Nature's offerings will prevail.

When descending, it's precipitation.

On the rise, it's evaporation.

Hence, that's the water cycle.

Holiday Recollections

Building a snowman from fallen snow

The mercury in a downward flow

Ornamented evergreens with flashing

Lights

Distant stars illuminating chilly nights

Listening to spirited holiday chatter

Sampling Mama's delicious cake batter

Silver and gold, red, white and green

A splendidly festive color scheme

Sleigh bells sharply jingling, jingling

Caroling voices melodiously singing

Delightful aromas of traditional dishes

Mile long lists of children's wishes

Eve gatherings with family and friends

Season's greetings everyone extends

Fun and laughter and big bear hugs

Eggnog and cider poured from jugs

Wreaths decorating windows and doors

An exchange of presents by the scores

A real treasure trove of wonderful toys

For the worthy girls and worthy boys

Songs of Santa and reindeer on the go

Hanging stockings and lucky mistletoe

Yule logs crackling in fireplaces

Expressed happiness adorning all faces

Alas, little ones sent off early to their beds

Too much merriment affecting their heads

Milk and cookies left for Old Saint Nick

In the wake of one lit candlestick

Christmas morning a quick leap from bed

An under tree search before being fed

A show of appreciation for gifts received

Just what was wanted, all so relieved

What wonderful recollections of holidays

Gone by!

LIMERICKS

A limerick is a humorous, rhyming five-line poem. It has a specific meter and rhyme scheme. Usually there are three strong stresses in lines 1,2, and 5 and two strong stresses in lines 3 and 4.

An old lady once lived down the road

    Until she invited home a plump toad.

        To her shock and utter dismay,

            She suddenly had no place to stay.

                Frog eggs were being laid by the load.

                    There once was a man named Aubrey

            That attempted to swat a flea

        Then he opened his mouth quite wide

      And suddenly choked and died

When down his throat flew a bee.

There is news of the man, John Devin

    Who never could count to seven

        Until his children totaled six,

            Taught John to count sticks.

                Now John Devin can count to eleven.

Sebastian Bates, the meanest of men,

    Peered in a well, then tumbled in.

        No one was concerned that he fell

            Until he commenced to scream and yell,

                Alarming the town again and again.

                    Those proper ladies of Cabbage Patch Lane

            Declare their ardent desire for rain.

        Yet, when hearing the slightest little drop

    Touch down upon any housetop,

Inconsolably, they rant, rave, and complain.

Otis Peabody grew up in the Town of O'Tool

    Where he played hooky, daily from school.

        Certainly, it was a known fact

            He was guilty of the act

                Is why today, he's called the town fool.

Stingy old Farmer Mac Duff

    Never fed his animals nearly enough.

        So early one very opportune day,

            The animals caught the old miser away,

                Ate everything, then waited for Mac Duff in a huff.

                Those Delany boys, though just a few,

            Were always such a troublesome crew,

        Told all the lies they could,

      Much more than they should,

'Til their noses grew and grew and grew.

The new schoolmaster has the look of a clown

    Due to an unusual facial frown

        That discourages any audible laughter

            During his presence and even after.

                Could it be, the frown is his smile upside-down?

An old friend was given a name

    Of which he is mighty a shame

        Even though he holds no malice

            When he is loudly called Alice,

                He responds to it just the same.

                There once was a man called Samuel Tappy

            Who had no intention of ever being happy.

        He married thrice in one life

      The very same mean, nagging wife

    A consequence of acting too snappy.

A city slicker approached what he thought was a cow

    Found himself splashing down by the side of a sow.

        What he vividly remembered of that terrible day

            Were the loud squeals of a dozen piglets as he lay

                Faced down in mud to the top of each brow.

In the small Iris town of Kildare

    Lived an old widower and his mare.

        Because the horse was dressed as a clown

            Whenever she was taken to town

                The locals doubted the man was all there.

                An extremely frazzled merchant name Sally

            Spent vast amounts of time in an ally

        Chasing her pet chimpanzee

      She affectionately called Friccazee,

Where he met others to chew the fat and dilly dally.

When Billy Sweeney's old yellow cat

    Lost his tail in pursuit of a rat,

        He switched to a diet of crickets and bugs

            And defenseless slow-slithering slugs

                Though he craved bigger prey with more fat.

Mickey O'Malley just down from Leeds

    Unaware he had swallowed seeds,

        Developed the weirdest appetite

            For soil, water, and sunlight,

                Was mortified when both ears sprouted weeds.

                In a dream, Turner Greer down on his luck

            Sent his frail wife to earn a buck

        While home and ten children he agreed to keep

      Suddenly bolted upright out of his sleep

To stop his life running a muck.

There was once a town name Tompkins Glenn

    Where people stalked the ghost of one, Peter O'Flynn

        'Til the angered spirit reversed the tide

            Spiraling them up in a tornado like ride.

                Now deservingly so, it's Ben Dun N.

www.ingramcontent.com/pod-product-compliance
Lightning Source LLC
Chambersburg PA
CBHW071505070526
44578CB00001B/450